Unleash the Power of You

A Step-by-Step Guide to Creating and Sustaining Your Own Personal Brand

D1488748

Also by Valerie Nifora

I Asked the Wind: A Collection of Romantic Poetry
The Fairmounts (Book 1)
Mary Whitcombe (The Fairmounts series Book 2)

Unleash the Power of You

A Step-by-Step Guide to Creating and Sustaining Your Own Personal Brand

VALERIE NIFORA

ethos
collective

Published by Ethos Collective™
PO Box 43, Powell, OH 43065
EthosCollective.vip

LCCN: 2023902499
Paperback ISBN: 978-1-63680-125-4
Hardback ISBN: 978-1-63680-126-1
e-book ISBN: 978-1-63680-127-8
Available in paperback, hardback, and e-book

Photographs by Duane Hodge.

DEDICATION

For Alan–
My North Star
My Always

If you're not branding yourself,
you can be sure others do it for you.

—Unknown

CONTENTS

FOREWORD

My name is Heather Monahan, and I am a two-time best-selling author, board member, top podcast host, and was named among the Top 50 Keynote Speakers in the World for 2022. But things have not always been roses and rainbows.

When I finally made it to the C-suite in corporate America, I thought things were going to get easier. I was wrong. What I didn't realize is, when you are employed by someone else you are subject to whatever changes occur at the company.

The CEO I worked for became ill suddenly, and he chose his daughter to replace him. That changed the course of my life. Overnight I went from one of the top executives in media to unemployed. It can happen that fast and yes, it is awful. However, I took that opportunity to reinvent myself. This is why personal branding is so important, and why Valerie Nifora's book is a great way to get you started.

People thought I was crazy for attempting to reinvent myself, so I tuned out the noise and tuned into myself. At first, everyone asks why you're doing it. Later they all ask how you did it.

Here's how I did it:

- When I got fired at forty-three years old, I decided to shine a light on it.
- I decided to reframe getting fired as *In Good Company!*

- I researched successful people who had been fired and found a big list that included J.K. Rowling, Steve Jobs, and Mark Cuban, to name a few.
- Then I posted about it:

> "After fourteen years of continuous advancement, I have just been fired. If I have ever done anything to help you, I would love to hear from you now."

That post went viral and Froggy from the Elvis Duran show tweeted at me, "How can I help?" One thing I had learned was to convert offers for help into opportunities *in the moment*. I tweeted back, "Book me on the show," and he did. I didn't know what we would talk about, but I knew I would reach a larger audience that would help me expand my network. Halfway through the show, Elvis said to me, "Obviously, you are writing a book!"

I smiled and agreed. The funny thing is I wasn't writing a book until Elvis told me I was. In that moment, he passed his belief in me to me, and I ran with it. I had no idea how to write a book, so I googled it. Turns out the key is just to sit down and write. Listen to yourself and your ideas over everything. Believe in them wholeheartedly. If you don't, why would anyone else? Accept feeling scared. Doing so allows the fear to pass.

Change represents a loss of some kind and letting go of familiar is exactly the loss you need. You must let go of mediocre if you want to grab great. Protect your ideas early on when they are the most vulnerable. I didn't tell anyone I was writing my first book, *Confidence Creator*, until I was done.

Take massive action and no matter what obstacles you meet just keep going. You will begin to see the dots connect if you don't give up on you.

I am not giving up either.

Don't give up on you and make sure you overcome your villains. We either overcome them or they overtake us. The choice is yours. Choose wisely.

–Heather Monahan
Best-selling Author of *Overcome Your Villains*

THE BEGINNING OF REINVENTION

It started out just like any other day. I logged into my computer to see what calls I had and started to go down the list of things I needed to accomplish when I got an instant message from my manager to call her. I did, not thinking much of it, and then the worst happened.

There was a long silence at the end of the line. There was no, "Hi. How are you?" Just a deep breath and a prepared speech she started to read me. Something or other about resource sizing and how there was a package. I remember interrupting her and saying, "Wait. You're laying me off?" I remember staring out the window at the leaves blowing through the trees. It wasn't her decision. She wasn't consulted. And, if memory serves, I think I actually tried to comfort *her*.

But there it was. Seventeen years of faithful and loyal service reduced to a seven-minute conversation that required me to read through an email, fill out paperwork, and look for an overnight package. What unfolded, as a result, was a fantastic journey that led me to writing this book. It's time all of us take control over the power we have as individuals.

Your career journey is your responsibility, and it starts with knowing who you are and what you want. That's not to say that can't change over time, but you, and no one else, own your destiny. The first step in this journey is to create and then sustain your own personal brand.

We may have all heard that expression, and probably feel that it's important (otherwise why would you be reading this book right now?), but HOW you do it is an art. Over my twenty-five plus years, I've helped shape and evolve many personal brands. In this book, I show you how to do this, step by step. By the end of this book, you'll have learned to create and sustain your own personal brands.

Remember: You either manage your personal brand or someone else will do it for you.

CHAPTER 1

You Are Unique

One of my college professors reminded each student in the class, almost daily, that each of us was unique. He would say the universe assembled all the DNA strands and molecules together to create each of us—once. And only, once. No other person on the planet would have our unique experiences, perspectives, interpretations, and thought processes. Even identical twins were different in how they perceive and experienced the world. His perspective made us believe we were special and our lives were important. Sitting there as a young college student, I wondered what in the world that had to do with anything, but I get it now.

There will always be someone who might be smarter, younger, faster, or more eager than you, but what you have to offer the world is *you*. The way you interpret the events in your life. The way you move forward in the face of success or failure. The way you envision solutions or even the way you solve problems is unique to *you*. You are the world's greatest asset. You have no duplicate, and there is no one who will be able to approach things exactly like you. What does all this mean?

It means successful people are those who can fully understand and realize the aspects that make them unique. And they use this knowledge to help them achieve their goals, dreams, ambitions, and desires. It means if you take a moment to fully consider your strengths and weaknesses, you'll begin to figure out what attributes will help you get where you need to go and allow you to take steps to ensure your weaknesses aren't going to sabotage your success. For example, if you gamble, steal, lie, or are intoxicated on a regular basis, you might want to consider getting some help for that first. If your weaknesses involve poor organization skills or difficulty managing multiple projects, mitigate those weaknesses as much as you can, but don't make them your sole focus. Instead, identify your strengths and develop those as much as possible.

Perhaps you're a creative thinker. Maybe you solve problems quickly and carefully. Maybe you're able to take the emotion out of a situation and see things with a clear and cool head. Work on those. Take courses, read books, and find mentors who will help you grow, develop, and strengthen those skills. The things you do well, these strengths, will help create the basic elements from which you will build your own personal brand. When you combine these strengths with all the experiences, perspectives, and solutions that make you such a unique force in the world, you can be assured your brand will be unlike any other because you are not like anyone else.

Abraham Lincoln once said, "Character is like a tree and the reputation is like its shadow. The shadow is what we think of it; the tree is the real thing." What I want you to contemplate is the actual tree. Go ahead. Picture a tree in your head. Got it? Hold on to that image. Now, add a light source, like the sun, and picture the shadow. Now move that light source around a little bit in your imagination. What is happening to the shadow? The shadow will change depending on the direction of the sun. That shadow represents what other people think of you. These impressions might change over time depending on people's experiences with your work or with you as a person.

The tree, what you are at your core, will not change. That which makes you unique will remain regardless of the finicky nature of people's impressions of you. The various elements of the tree—the bark, leaves, limbs—are the building blocks of what the tree is, and subsequently, distinguish this tree from any other tree. Those basic and defining elements are what you will use to build your brand. They reflect the many distinct parts of you. When you capture those elements to share with the world, do so honestly and genuinely, and you'll be able to weather any lengthening or shortening of shadows that might come to pass.

Billionaire Richard Branson once remarked, "Your brand name is only as good as your reputation." While I'm a firm believer in trying to build the best reputation possible for yourself and your brand, not everyone is going to jump on board and respect it. There will be people who will try to tarnish your reputation or dispute your credibility or question your integrity, and their efforts might be based on fact or fiction. Remember: Reputation is simply an impression of brand. It's that shadow of the tree we imagined earlier. If you build your brand on things that don't rely solely on reputation, you'll be able to withstand the figurative storm of misrepresentation or misgivings.

> The brand you build should be created on a solid foundation of attributes that are *real* and *authentic* to you.

The brand you build should be created on a solid foundation of attributes that are *real* and *authentic* to you. For example, if you genuinely don't care about what happens in your colleagues' personal lives at work, then compassion, is probably not a brand element you want to attribute to yourself. If you are one of those people who worries about everything that happens to your colleagues—right down to sick pets—compassion might be a dimension of your personal brand. Like a Hollywood celebrity, you could always create a brand based on a fleeting fad or persona that might or might not be real, but if you're reading this book, you're not likely a celebrity with a high-paid publicist trying to help you get your next movie deal. You are reading this book to help piece together how to optimize the characteristics that make you unique. To that end, let's take a deep breath and dive right in.

How Unique Are We?

In a 2011 TEDx Talk, self-help author Mel Robbins announced that the odds of being born are **one in 400 trillion.**

Each person has twenty-three pairs of chromosomes and can produce 8,388,608 different gametes—our reproductive cells. Taking this one step further, the possible combinations that emerge from the pairing of an egg and a sperm the result in $(2^{23})^2$ **possible combinations, or more than 70 trillion.**

"The universe of genes that are actually expressed in humans—called the exome—is comprised of about 30 million bases of DNA," according to Drew Smith.

There are 7 billion humans, so we know some 420 billion different variants are possible.

Personal Story: Here's the Thing

I grew up as the only Greek American in my class, and there were very few of us in my school. My parents were first-generation immigrants, and I had a hard time with English because it wasn't the language I learned first.

I was fairly intelligent and had a lovely imagination. I always told stories. I wasn't shy. And I wasn't the best at picking up social cues that invited me to simply be quiet.

In short, I was different. But aren't we all?

I could probably spend the next few pages telling you about being bullied as a child and young adult. These "bullies" ran the gamut from family members to "friends" to classmates. Each with their own idea of what I was supposed to be. But I'm going to pass on that. I think each of us has felt bullied in one way or another, and besides, the topic was probably already covered in many after-school specials. Yes, I ate most of my lunches alone, but here's the thing—I didn't mind. Honestly. I just read, or wrote, or did my homework, or stared into space. Solitude is greatly undervalued.

The general criticism was that I was *too* something—too loud, too creative, too dramatic, too smart, too aggressive. You get the idea. The reality, however, was *I was just the right amount of whatever it was.* You are too.

What got me through life was my younger sister, my incredible champion. Although we have nothing in common, she thought I was just the right amount of whatever it was too. In some ways, we're total opposites. I'm viewed as loud and outgoing, and my sister is quiet

> I'm here to tell you that you are unique, special, a one-of-a-kind human, with a one-of-a-kind mix of extraordinary skills, capabilities, and experience.

and reserved—at least until you get to know her, and then you see where the boundaries blur.

I'm not sure who might have told you differently, *but I'm here to tell you that you are unique, special, a one-of-a-kind human, with a one-of-a-kind mix of extraordinary skills, capabilities, and experience.* You have a lot to offer the world. I'm here to help you unlock it.

Let's get started.

You Do You

Guest Column by Dr. Stacy Feiner

Human beings are born with an innate tension between the need to belong and the desire to be an individual. These two psychological needs are inescapably intertwined, and the interplay between them underpins everything we do. How we reconcile this internal tension shapes who we are, the relationships we form, and how we live our lives.

In the best case, this tension sparks growth and makes it possible to adapt and progress on a healthy developmental trajectory. But what if our individuality challenges the status quo, threatens the norms of our social group, and puts us at risk for being rejected and ridiculed? By the same token, what if the comfort of acceptance and safety ensnares us in peer pressure and dulls the fever to find our own voice and pursue our unique purpose?

We spend our entire lives navigating our need to belong in tandem with our need for self-expression. We are always looking for where we can find safety, acceptance, and love, while simultaneously fulfilling the desire to be unique and express our own experience of the world around us, our ideas, and purpose. As we set sail through life, we require different amounts of belonging and self-expression.

As a psychologist, it's fundamental to tap into this unexplored tension and engage it as a natural resource of energy to help people discover the reservoir of potential embedded within it. Using psychology as the lens, precious insights, emotions, and dynamics reveal the unique facets within each of us.

Most people are very unpracticed at drawing on their individuality for growth, opting instead to retreat when discoveries take too long, feel too challenging, or require too much. Growth, I've come to understand, happens when we explore the boundaries of our uniqueness.

Like everything worth having, becoming our whole selves takes time, introspection, exploration, experimentation, as well as interaction, collaboration, and connection. A willingness to visit ineffective and stifling patterns of the past and an unwavering dedication to breaking through them. Each of us can level up our performance for ourselves and those in our sphere once we redirect that which was misassigned as a negative and use it to discover our unique competitive advantage.

It's amazing how often perceived negative traits have roots in our uniqueness which were long ago a threat to belonging. Rather than saddling ourselves with punishing labels, uniqueness is essential for purpose, growth, ambition, and pursuit of our full capacity.

Our quirks are what make us captivating, motivating, and profoundly influential. What it takes is a commitment to self-acceptance and emotional awareness. Acceptance of our individuality is an inside job and embracing your uniqueness means you leapfrog obstacles and embrace the masterpiece within, whether tendencies come naturally or need guidance through the emotional excavation process. There are many paths, and all require the time to purposefully stack the mini wins, celebrate setbacks as steppingstones, and fail forward. Exploration of the tension is foundational to understanding and accepting ourselves. After all, you are the most qualified to do you.

About the Contributor

Dr. Stacy Feiner is a nationally recognized innovative psychologist known for leveling-up the output of elite performers and the complex systems they lead. Using the lens of psychology, Dr. Feiner taps the invisible dynamics that make people tick and groups click. In your ear and at your side, Dr. Feiner coaches you to achieve the results you want in all areas of your life.

Try It Out!

What makes you unique? Share three qualities or quirks you think make you stand out. (There are no wrong answers!)

1. _____
2. _____
3. _____

What are the values and beliefs that will shape your contribution to the world?

1. _____
2. _____
3. _____

What are the skills and talents that will shape your contribution?

1. _____
2. _____
3. _____

What you have learned in this chapter:

- ✓ You're unique.
- ✓ You have a guideline of what makes you special.
- ✓ Your strengths are your greatest assets.

CHAPTER 2

Defining Your Brand

What is a brand? Often when we ask this question, images of logos, products, commercials, print ads, and jingles will come flooding into our minds. In the strictest of dictionary definitions, a brand is a type of product manufactured by a particular company under a particular name. A quick search on *Wikipedia* brings forth the following: Branding is a set of marketing and communications methods that help to distinguish a company from competitors and create an impression in the minds of customers. So now you might ask, *What in the world does that have to do with me?*

You are the product of your years of professional experience, education, training, and employment. You have a set of skills and knowledge that is unique to anyone else sitting next to you. How you work, who you know, what you know, and what you produce all distinguish you from your competitors. You are a product. People buy *you* when an employer hires you to do a certain job or assigns you to a certain project. Your professional self is a brand—brand YOU.

In this book, we will explore how to discover your brand and define it in a way that sets you apart from your competitors and creates an impression in the minds of your employers and colleagues (customers).

> Your professional self is a brand—brand YOU.

Close your eyes for a second and visualize your favorite brand. Does it have a logo? What color is the logo? Do you use the product? How do you use it or interact with it? Why do you use it? How does it make you feel? The answers to those questions are your perceptions of that brand, and those perceptions help shape the brand's attributes. That's the shadow we discussed in the previous chapter. There are also tangible aspects about the product—quality, shape, color—that will not change. Whether or not another product might meet your needs better doesn't matter because you selected a specific product for this exercise. It is what you believe about the product and how you feel about it, and why you use it that matters most. All those elements together help inform what you will perceive of the brand. It is what marketers have spent time and money crafting and refining, to get you, as part of a specific target audience, to buy that product or service.

Abraham H. Maslow, an American psychologist and philosopher, developed the idea that all human actions are based on a hierarchy of needs. His theory is often depicted as a five-tiered pyramid with the most basic needs—food, drink, shelter, relief from pain—comprising the base and the more intangible needs—friendship, self-esteem, self-expression—making up the top tiers. Effective product marketers figure out where their products fit into this pyramid and then build specific messaging to reach consumers most likely to purchase based on the desire to fill that need.

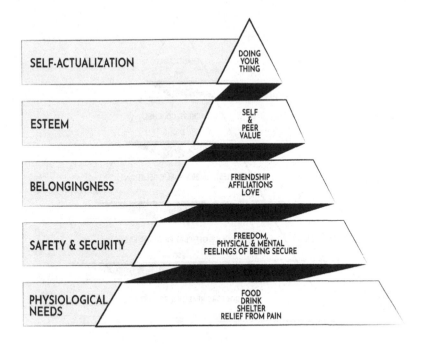

When you think of yourself as a product, it's helpful to determine which of those needs you can best meet. How does your background or your experiences fit within Maslow's hierarchy of needs pyramid? Do your skills help meet the need for shelter, food, clothing? Does your occupation help others achieve a higher level of self-esteem through educational services or coaching? Take a moment to contemplate each tier of the pyramid and where you feel where your profession would fall within the diagram.

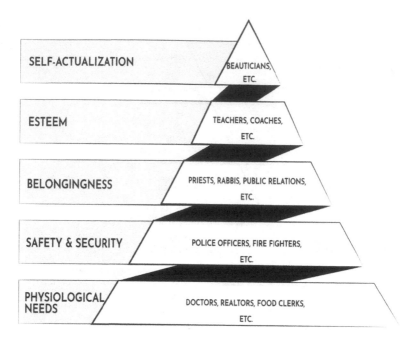

How people perceive your brand and how they feel about your ability to deliver on your skills constitutes the brand promise. You might wonder when it was that you ever put together a promise about what you could deliver. You did it, chances are unconsciously, when you put together your resume or built your LinkedIn profile, your Facebook page, your Twitter account or some other online or social media presence. Every time you post an article, retweet a quote or simply put up a picture, you are curating your brand. As a result, people are creating an impression of who you are, what you're about, and what you might be able to deliver. My goal with this book is to help you create a thoughtful and intentional brand promise.

Personal Story: Don't Be a Jerk

I've lived in the corporate world for almost three decades. It's okay—I started when I was five. (Anyone else hear the drum roll?) During my time, I've had incredible experiences with amazing people, some of whom are featured in this book, and other unfortunate experiences with some not-so-awesome people.

These not-so-awesome people were the throw-you-under-the-bus-to-get-ahead crowd. They were the sort who miraculously suffered amnesia right after you came to an agreement because the political wind was no longer blowing in the direction of the decision you mutually made. Anyone else ever caught in that gale? I'm not embarrassed to say I have a running list of people I won't work with again. You probably do, too.

When it comes to the people in the *amazing* group, I have learned to value the following: generosity, talent, positivity, encouragement, unwavering spirit, and a desire to raise others up. It's been said that your vibe attracts your tribe, and I am so fortunate to be a member of such an incredible tribe, which, of course, you are welcome to join.

As you start to create your personal brand, think of what you want to represent in five years, ten years, twenty years, thirty years

> Your vibe attracts your tribe.

from now? What will be your legacy? A friend of mine, who I would call crying every time one of these not-so-nice folks tried to run me over, always reminded me of this saying: *You can climb over as many people as you want on the way up the ladder, but don't be surprised if they step aside when you miss a rung and go sliding down.*

Life is short. Don't be a jerk.

The Power of Little Brands

Guest Column by Dave Carlquist

Iconic brands have big names, powerful reputations, and represent incredible value in the marketplace. Big Brands like Apple®, Coca Cola®, Google®, and McDonald's® are recognizable around the world and conjure in our minds a strong value proposition, a respected set of qualities, and a central purpose.

It is not just large enterprises that forge and value their brands. Individuals from all walks of life all over the world build, promote, and protect their own personal brands in much the same way. These Little Brands are less popular than the billion-dollar household names, but they still represent who these people are and what they hold important.

> It is not just large enterprises that forge and value their brands. Individuals from all walks of life all over the world build, promote, and protect their own personal brands.

But how do individuals properly define their personal brands? It can happen via serendipity like sedimentary rock formed by randomly deposited by air, wind, or water. Individuals create the most effective brands when they mine their personal narratives and build a solid foundation made up of values, priorities, personality quirks, learned skills, and lifelong dreams. Combining those elements with everyday practical and professional experience over an extended period of time is what defines a brand. Being intentional is critical because an intentionally shaped brand is one that is built to last.

In my case, I spent my entire career, nearly thirty-seven years, working hard for IBM®, also known as "Big Blue." IBM is a respected brand easily identified by its eight-bar logo and known for service ("IBM Means Service"), technology, innovation (global leader in new patents), and talent (the IBMer).

As an executive, I would often repeat that IBM's greatest invention ever was the IBMer. My colleagues, supported by the company's culture, were a formidable workforce. Logos and slogans might symbolize a brand, but it's the collective action and contributions of the organization's individuals that ultimately define the Big Brand. In IBM's case, it was the technology along with the nearly 400,000 employees plus business partners who defined the brand.

I had the privilege of working with many extraordinary people at IBM, the best of the best. I not only fulfilled my role and did what was expected, I worked hard to excel. Instead of competing with colleagues, I tried to complement my team, align with IBM's interests, and provide value. Defining my personal brand wasn't mutually exclusive with the work at hand, but it was a priority. Why was it important?

- It provided differentiation across tens of thousands of colleagues.
- It was a reputational statement of my work product quality, similar to the Good Housekeeping Seal of Approval.
- It established what managers' and colleagues' expectations of me should be.
- It helped me define skill and experience gaps that needed to be addressed.
- It aided me in making choices and setting priorities.

Here are some examples of elements I emphasized in my personal brand:

Stewardship: As a team member, manager, and executive, I strove to be a "servant leader," choosing to prioritize others ahead of my self-interests which, ultimately, helped me with my goals. (A servant-leader focuses primarily on the growth and well-being of people and the communities to which they belong. While traditional leadership generally involves the accumulation and exercise of power by one at the "top of the pyramid," servant leadership is different. The servant-leader shares power, puts the needs of others first, and helps people develop and perform as highly as possible.)

Technical Leadership: Maintaining an above average technical aptitude added value and better served clients and colleagues. Being the technical geek would become a badge of honor that differentiated me from the rest of the field.

Humor: Infusing humor to de-stress serious work, lighten moods, and destabilize threatening situations was an asset. Whether it was writing and performing parody sketches in meetings or invoking sound effects in conference calls, levity helped me stand out, improve communications, and motivate others to work with me.

White Space: By tackling the hard yards—the business units or tasks that were either troubled or those that were new, unstructured, and in need of formation and direction—positioned me as someone that could be confidently plugged into new challenges.

It's never too late or too early to go to work defining or redefining your Little Brand. Here's how to start:

- Define the destination. Be intentional.
- Assess skills and capabilities, and plug gaps where necessary through formal education, experience building, or mentoring.
- Develop your narrative and leverage strengths and unique qualities.
- Talk is cheap. Find ways to prove your value.

- Be authentic. Trust is critical in forming a Big Brand and even more so as an individual. What are people saying about you when you aren't in the room? What's your reputation and what aspects of your reputation do you want featured?

Could I have done a better job at defining my brand and delivering against those expectations? Most likely. Do I wish I had had a copy of this book to guide me on the journey? Of course. When I look back, I consider these three KPIs, or key performance indicators, as affirmation of some level of success:

Personal Relationships: I was fortunate to have a nearly nineteen-year working relationship with the same executive assistant, practically unheard of at IBM where people changed roles as often as the weather in my hometown of Chicago. It was a productive and meaningful working relationship that strengthened my brand but was also a proof point of reputational success.

Career Longevity: It is increasingly rare that one's career can be charted from entry-level to senior executive at a single firm. I started as a systems engineer trainee and retired as an executive at one of the most respected companies in the world. Reputation and personal brand were critical success factors in that journey.

Career Accomplishments: When the Little Brand aligns with an organization's Big Brand qualities and the strategic intent of both is congruent, there is a virtuous cycle of complementary impacts and reinforcing experiences. In my case, my desire to work on client business problems, help build a smarter planet, be on the vanguard of technological innovations, and work with some of the best and brightest people on earth was right in line with the nature of the Big Brand for which I worked.

To the extent that legacy is fundamental to what it is to be human, creating a positive legacy can give great meaning to a life. But a legacy is often a single snapshot that is reflective of someone's entire body of work or lifetime of impact. Our personal brands are dynamic. They reflect the kind of people we want to be, the impact we want to have, and the potential we possess. They also help shape the future and attract opportunities.

Valerie's insights and the actions you can take to unleash the power of you starts with recognizing the power of your personal brand, intentionally setting your brand's design, and working diligently to reinforce it.

About the Contributor

Dave Carlquist is a board member and retired senior technology executive who spent more than thirty-six years with the IBM Corporation. During that time, he led a significant portion of U.S. sales, oversaw IBM's global systems channel business, and retired in the role of Vice President, Strategy, and Transformation. In that role, he was responsible for strategy and business transformation in support of client relationship management and sales engagement in IBM's largest client segment worldwide.

Try It Out!

Look at your resume, LinkedIn profile, or a recent cover letter. Based on those pieces, list three things that you are promising to deliver if someone were to hire you:

1. _____
2. _____
3. _____

Look at a one of your social media profiles. List the last three things you posted:

1. _____
2. _____
3. _____

What do these posts say about you? How do they align with or depart from the first three promises you listed?

_____
_____
_____
_____
_____

Where does your profession fit into Maslow's hierarchy of needs?

_____
_____
_____
_____
_____

What you have learned in this chapter:

✓ Where your profession fits in Maslow's Hierarchy of Needs.

✓ A clearer definition of your promise.

✓ Whether your posts align with your promise.

CHAPTER 3

Core Elements of Your Brand

Now that we have talked about what we mean by a brand, let's start thinking about pulling together the core elements of your brand. This chapter will serve as a guide for you to refocus and refine all the wonderful, complicated pieces that are you. We all have a particular perception of ourselves. If I asked you to complete this sentence, "I am...," you would start listing attributes.

Do that right now. Think of the adjectives you would use to describe yourself. Now think of the adjectives that others might use to describe you. And this is important—limit yourself to positive responses. You might be wondering why I am having you focus only on the positive, and that's because positivity—whether in descriptors, perspectives, or points of view—allows a person to aspire to something greater. People also gravitate to things that make them feel good. It can be helpful to think of all the positive adjectives you came up with as a bright light you're projecting into the world. Those points of light are your strengths, and as I mentioned earlier, I'm a fan of highlighting a person's strengths, not their weaknesses. You can skip ahead to page 31 and start writing down those adjectives and descriptors and then come back to read the rest.

The Power of a Word Cloud

If you already have a social media profile such as LinkedIn with recommendations or have access to your performance reviews, we're going to use those to help you build a word cloud. A word cloud is a visual depiction of the words used most frequently to describe you as a professional. This visual description makes the words most frequently used appear bigger than any other. Now, select a few sentences, copy, and paste those sentences into any website or software product that can create a word cloud. If you're not aware of one, I suggest using wordclouds.com or something similar.

As you look at your word cloud, note how many of the words match the positive adjectives you came up with a few minutes ago. This will give you an idea if you're on the right track in terms of your branding. If they're similar, you're in good shape. If they're not, now is the time to do some soul searching. *What do I want to be? What do I want others to think of me? What do I want to stand for?*

Take the word cloud and look for your descriptors. Circle the positive adjectives most frequently used in the word cloud. Find the two or three nouns most frequently used in the word cloud and circle those. Think back to your initial list of positive adjectives. Do they correlate?

Next look at those nouns. Did you associate yourself with a job? Did you associate yourself with a familial role? (For example: mom, parent, aunt, and others.)

Now take a pause. Think about if you want your personal brand to reflect those nouns, and how those nouns and adjectives match up.

I'm going to take a sidebar here to illustrate a point. I was working with a very senior executive once on his biography for a particular event. He said to me that everyone kept saying he needed to talk about his wife and his children in his bio. I asked him if he wanted to talk about that part of his life, and his answer was a resounding, "No." So, I told him to leave it out and it didn't matter what other people said to him.

When you craft your personal brand, don't emphasize roles you *don't* want to talk about. If you don't want to invite questions about being a working mother, for example, then don't talk about it on social media or at work. Otherwise, questions or commentary will come and you should expect both. Remember, you're completely allowed to keep whatever you want private and not part of your professional personal brand.

Now let's go back and look at the nouns and the adjectives in that word cloud. Do they match up? Are there any that are out of place? Do you agree with the assessment?

Now that you have an idea of what your brand is about, we're going to use your initial adjectives to build a statement. Fill them in as you complete the sentence again, "I am (your adjectives)" and add the job function. There's space for you to do this on page 32.

This will now be your brand statement, for example this is mine, "I am an innovative, enthusiastic and collaborative marketing strategist."

I absolutely love word clouds. They provide clarity as you start to craft and refine your brand. They're also a great way to check in to make sure what you want to emulate is actually coming through in your actions and others' impressions of you. Below is a word cloud based on feedback I received. After I aggregated the information, it made me smile.

using terms

closely adopt

organzation innovation

professional absolute excellent

services absolute

Branding wonderful

channels ideas first

concepts ever

person establishing

go-to

team communications

sometimes strengths

Valerie variety

describe simple

operating together chat excels

area capability

marketing helping

forum job organizations

new often storytelling

bring

difficult joy something

emerging worked strategic

example twitter

technologies

Personal Story: It's Not Really You

I'll never forget when I was up for a promotion and was denied. My manager at the time had done her due diligence and secured all the approvals from management. The last step was to secure the agreement of the vice president of the business unit I was supporting. We both felt confident it would happen.

She sat down with him and started to list my accomplishments and her support of my promotion. He interrupted with, "I think that Valerie is intimidating to the junior members of the team."

Silence. Neither my manager nor I expected that response. We were ill-prepared, and it was clear from his statement he was not signing off on my promotion. I figured it was a lost cause, I took a deep breath and said, "Well, I can't erase all these years of success or the awards I earned, and if people feel intimidated by me, I'm thinking that's more a problem with your leadership than my performance." Anyone else hear the mic drop?

My exceptional manager found me another position somewhere outside of that business unit with a new group of people who weren't intimidated. We both realized there was no point in supporting that business unit any longer. I moved on to a new team who embraced me and my skills with open arms. (Learning moment: never stay where you're undervalued.) And in case you're curious, yes, his commentary/reasoning for not extending me a promotion was 100 percent unconscious bias. How many men do you know are denied a promotion for being perceived as intimidating? I think most are rewarded.

> Don't let someone else define or limit you.

Fast-forward a few years, and I'm an award-winning poet, best-selling author, and global marketing leader who decided to share my knowledge with you, so you can excel.

Don't let someone else define or limit you.

Claim your brand attributes before someone else does it for you.

Incidentally, the flip side of intimidating is impactful. I choose to define myself as impactful.

Be a Lifelong Learner

Guest Column by Ben Amaba, PhD

When I started my career years ago, I never would have expected at this point in my life, I would have published more than thirty notable articles, hold two patents, a copyright, serve on several academic and research boards, and worked as the chief technology officer for one of the most influential Fortune 50 technology companies in the world. What I had was a natural interest in engineering with business and a desire to improve, grow, and take on as many challenges as I could and succeed. Life, they say, favors the brave, and I'll add hard-working.

I did have a core set of values. I was honest, trustworthy, and always willing to learn. You could say that early on I was a diligent student committed to success and learning from others. That's been a cornerstone of my entire career. Over time, additional pieces would fuse together as new experiences and opportunities came together all to facilitate growth.

I believe in helping others succeed. I believe in collaboration. I believe in reaching out and teaching the power and value of science and engineering with business.

In addition to my day job, I teach, lecture, keynote, and sit on several boards so I can pay my success forward. I encourage my twins and others to lean into STEM as a key mechanism to help shape the future of public health, safety, security, and the environment. There is a great opportunity for growth and change in the world, and we always need smart, passionate, and committed engineers, professionals, and innovators to create the next level of possible.

If I were to give advice, it would be this: stay true to your beliefs and the core of who you are as a person. Surround yourself with talented, compassionate, and ethical human beings. Dream and then find a way to make those dreams possible. Always be willing to try something new. Innovation comes from new ideas, and innovation makes the difference.

About the Contributor

Ben Amaba holds a doctorate in industrial and systems engineering, a master's degree in engineering and operations, and a bachelor's degree in electrical engineering. He serves on numerous boards, including Dearborn Artificial Intelligence Research Center, Center of Advanced Supply Chain Management, Industry Council Advisor for the Project Production Institute, and executive advisory boards at the University of Miami, University of Houston, University of Central Florida, Texas A&M University, and Clemson University.

Try It Out!

Let's start pulling together the core elements of your brand. List ten adjectives that describe you:

1. _____
2. _____
3. _____
4. _____
5. _____
6. _____
7. _____
8. _____
9. _____
10. _____

Next, list five adjectives that you think someone else would use to describe you. (I appreciate that might be a bit difficult, so take your time.)

1. _____
2. _____
3. _____
4. _____
5. _____

Cross out anything you wrote down that's negative. Don't try to replace it with a better or more positive word—just cross it out entirely. If you find yourself without a list of positive words, go back and redo the exercise.

Merge your two lists into one, using only those positive words. This will be your starting point.

1. _____
2. _____
3. _____
4. _____
5. _____

List three nouns you see repeated.

1. _____
2. _____
3. _____

Now look at your list of merged adjectives. Do they correlate? Think of how you can think through those adjectives and nouns.

Write your "I am..." statement in the section below.

_____
_____
_____
_____
_____

Take some time to reflect on this chapter and this exercise before moving ahead.

What you have learned in this chapter:

✓ A better understanding of how people perceive you at the moment you're reading this book.

✓ An understanding of whether there's a gap between your perception and the perception of others.

✓ A clear "I am" statement that highlights your strengths with your job function.

✓ The beginning of your personal brand statement.

CHAPTER 4

Social Media and Your Brand

Just look around and it's clear that most of us are addicted to our smartphones and other electronic devices. As a matter of fact, the average person spends over three hours a day on their phone. I cannot tell you the number of times I've watched people walking around staring at their cell phones with absolutely no idea where they are going—simply walking into traffic while happily posting to Twitter and Facebook. It's absurd that we'd rather post a picture of a tree than sit underneath one. Whatever happened to enjoying the shade or watching the leaves dance in the wind? But I digress. What does this have to do with a personal brand. A lot!

I know of plenty of people who divide their social media vehicles into categories. They'll think, for example, that their professional social media platforms will be LinkedIn and Twitter. And their personal social media platforms will be Facebook, Snapchat, Tumblr, and Pinterest. Makes sense, right? I'm here to challenge that idea because every single time you post something on any social media vehicle, whether you delete it or not, it's there forever, cached into the ether. Every political view, statement, comment, argument, and photo will be there contributing to how people interpret who you are and by extension your brand. But wait, you argue, *I want to be authentic. I didn't like that picture, post, or article, and I should be able to say so. It's my voice.* Yes, it is. But recognize that every time you do so, you're contributing to the brand you're building for yourself. A brand that will be seen by those who know you and those who don't.

Consider interactions on Facebook. I'm often astounded by the personal things that people post there—and the audacious and impolite responses they receive from other people. I am stunned that people will post comments that they wouldn't dare utter if sitting across a table from the other person. It is certainly a beacon of the death of polite society.

My mom would always tell me to be cautious because you never know who knows who—and the same applies here. You never know if that post you made five years ago that was liked by someone in your network will be picked up by another party in another network and ultimately make its way to a future or potential boss or business partner. No matter how many privacy settings and safeguards we put in place, no social media platform is foolproof. Be mindful. In addition to employers, insurance companies, government agencies, colleagues, and family members, many others can potentially access your commentary, photographs, and memes, whether you intended them to be seen by such a vast audience or not.

> No matter how many privacy settings and safeguards we put in place, no social media platform is foolproof. Be mindful.

The first thing I do before I have a conversation with anyone I don't know is search for that person on social media. Whether it's a professional encounter or not, before I get on the phone, I do my best to know as much about that person as possible. I search Facebook, Twitter, LinkedIn, Pinterest—anything and everything I can get my hands on. I quickly start to assemble a profile of that person: where he went to school, what groups he associates with, what articles he's posted or written, what's he's liked or not like, what hobbies he has, etc. I have a good idea of who I'm going to be talking to and what that person is all about. Creepy? Possibly. But it's there to acquire—self-published for consumption. And if I'm doing it for someone who might want to pitch me a product or service at a business meeting, what do you think human resources departments are doing when your inquiry for a position comes their way?

Think about your key brand attributes. Are you compassionate? Then make a dedicated effort to express that in your social media engagements. Do you want to be known as a person who is an expert in his or her field? Share the latest articles that you've read and explain why you found them interesting. You don't have to lack authenticity, but you should have the good common sense to understand that virtual you and in-person you are one in the same. Social media can be a hindrance to your brand if you don't manage it properly.

Here's a check list of common social media vehicles and what to keep an eye out for as it relates to your brand:

Social Vehicle	Description	Common Pitfalls
Facebook (Meta)	Social networking site that enables the sharing of content. Originally intended for friends and family the platform has evolved to include many successful business pages. Users post content onto an individual page that can be viewed by members designated by the user or the public at large based on the configurations the user sets.	Little thought to content being provided. Response may be knee-jerk in nature. Commentary may be in appropriate or would not be said out loud if in person. Some material might be too personal for prime time.

LinkedIn	Professional networking platform which allows job seekers to post their CVs/resumes, apply for jobs and seek career development. Users are able to increase their network through connections as well as post and comment on content posted.	Treating the platform like it's Facebook (Meta). Make sure whatever you're posting is providing value to your network.
Twitter	Social networking service on which users post short messages and images known as tweets.	Negative comments or virtual bullying. Be mindful what you post. It lasts forever.
Pinterest	Pinterest is an image sharing and social media service which uses images, animated GIFs, and videos, in the form of pinboards.	Be mindful of the nature and consistency of images shared.
Tumblr	A microblogging and social networking service which allows users to post multimedia and other content to a short-form blog.	Make sure the content posted provides value. Make sure the content posted is consistent with your brand.

Snapchat	American multimedia instant messaging app. Messages are only available for a brief period of time before they become inaccessible.	Negative, mean, or inappropriate comments shared.
Instagram	Photo and video sharing (reels) social networking platform.	Inconsistent messaging or imagery. Unclear purpose in posting content.
TikTok	TikTok is a video-focused social networking service. It hosts a variety of short-form user videos ranging in genres from dance, comedy, education, reviews and more. Videos lengths vary from fifteen seconds to three minutes.	Offensive, inappropriate, or false content. Be mindful of spyware as that is part of the service.

Personal story: Trending on LinkedIn

LinkedIn is my favorite social platform. I understand it. I feel comfortable using it. I believe it provides incredible value to its users. I must not be the only one who feels this way about the platform, as there are more than 875 million users as of the printing of this book and no doubt will continue to grow.

I've had the great honor of trending a few times on LinkedIn. This is something that I'm particularly pleased about. Why should it matter? Because this has helped me expand my message and reinforce my brand to my audience.

By posting articles that are core to who I am as a professional and who I am as an individual, I'm able to find the audience that appreciates the value I bring. I receive requests for speaking engagements, training sessions, and roundtables. And, of course, recruiters have reached out, which is what makes this particular social platform so powerful for any professional.

It never hurts to have options.

You should have options, too.

Share Your Crayons

Guest Column by Doreen Marchetti

When I was in kindergarten, *social* meant something entirely different. It meant sharing your crayons and playing nicely with the other kids. Media was clearly defined as television, which for me, naturally meant *Mister Rogers' Neighborhood* all the way!

I was not an early adopter of what we define today as social media. Each platform I embraced filled the need for a specific point in time, to serve a specific audience, and for a specific purpose.

- Facebook, not until I was PTO Co-president to share events and information
- Twitter, not until my employer required tweets at events to increase awareness and reach
- LinkedIn, not until I sought a new career to find recruiters and hiring managers

I am not on TikTok, Instagram, or Snapchat. I have dabbled in Clubhouse.

My minimalistic but focused approach to social media is simple. It requires thought, time, and respect. And I purposefully curate what I will share on which platform keeping in mind what that audience needs.

What do I want my brand to be? I'd like to be known as someone who posts thoughtful, timely, and respectful content. Maybe this comes from my early learning from mom's mantra, "If you don't have something nice to say, don't say anything at all." I believe there is a way to say things that provoke discussion, not hatred, and gives a voice for a healthy debate.

My go-to platform is LinkedIn. Grown from a base of 500 (the minimum needed for a recruiting algorithm) to over 23,000 (and growing) connections with colleagues, valued Business Partners, professional friendships, and family members. Over the years, it has enriched my life with curiosity, content, people, and learning. I get inspired. I share. I inspire others.

When I look at a post, I look at who else has reacted. Posts are a great source of potential new connections, new people to learn from and to share with. Some people are like-minded, others promote different perspectives. I keep an eye on my notifications in the platform, as I enjoy sending birthday wishes and congratulatory notes on promotions and new roles. These interactions sometimes result in an unexpected reunion with a person from the past. But it's not only the connections but also who you follow, allowing for the discovery of new companies, cultures, and ways to think of the ordinary or not so ordinary.

> When I look at a post, I look at who else has reacted. It's a great source of potential new connections, new people to learn from and to share with.

I have been introduced to people I would otherwise never have had the opportunity to meet. I have learned interesting tidbits about my partners and clients and participated in webinars and events. I have built a community around other women in IT, and caregivers who share in the responsibility of helping someone with Parkinson's Disease. My brand on LinkedIn is important to me as it not only reflects who I am, but also my work, past and present. I guess you could say that I still like sharing my crayons.

Our journey on social might be best summed up with one of Mister Rogers' quotes:

"All of us, at some time or other, need help. Whether we're giving or receiving, each one of us has something valuable to bring to this world. That's one of the things that connects us as neighbors—in our own way, each of us is a giver and a receiver."

About the Contributor

Doreen Marchetti has spent more than thirty years in the IT industry, most notably at IBM where she built high performing teams and helped an extensive list of Ecosystem Partners exceed growth expectations. Sales, marketing, business development, and channel enablement roles took her to forty-four countries, managing and mentoring hundreds of employees. She has served as a board member, consultant, and dedicated mother and wife. Doreen's signature meatballs continue to be a fan favorite for anyone who's been fortunate enough to be invited to dinner.

Try It Out!

Take stock of your most frequently used social media platforms. Describe a few of your most recent posts. How do
they line up with your personal brand? How did they serve
your audience?

_____

_____

_____

_____

_____

Managing a social media presence for your brand can become
a full-time job. Fill out the chart below to give yourself some
guidelines on how you'll interact in social media.

Social Vehicle	Brand Aspect to Highlight	Types of Posts

What you have learned in this chapter:

✓ Be mindful of what you post on social media. It lasts forever.

✓ Boundaries in social media between "personal" and "professional" posts are rare.

✓ Know which of the social media vehicles you want to cultivate.

CHAPTER 5

Brand Life Cycle

If we take a moment and think of your brand as a reflection of the you as a product, we must consider for a moment that all products inevitably go through a typical product life cycle. These cycles include multiple stages including introduction, growth, maturity, and decline. And typically, so will your personal brand. Especially as you change careers or roles.

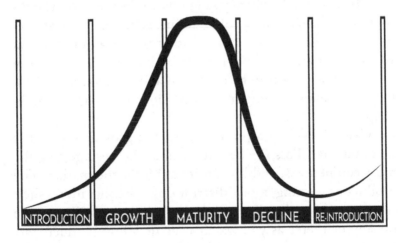

Given where you are in your career lifecycle, you might need to use different tactics to manage your brand. Let's look at the different stages and how to manage your brand in accordance with the appropriate stage.

Introduction: During the introduction phase, you are starting with a clean slate. At this stage, the great wide world has no impression or a small impression of what you're about as a professional. This is now the perfect opportunity to share all the elements of your brand. Go back and look at your brand statement. If we use the example, "I am an innovative, enthusiastic, and collaborative marketing strategist." Start using social media to highlight what you consider to be innovative as it relates to your career. Share what you are "enthusiastic" about, for example, coaching soccer or your interest in a particular artist. Here is when you start to decide how much of your personal interests and your personal life you are willing to share with the world.

When we look at the description of "collaborative" in the example "I am" statement above, you can talk about the membership you have in different associations and how you participate in them, or perhaps, you have projects you can talk about publicly where you are part of a team. Maybe it's something as simple as volunteering your time at a shelter or soup kitchen or whatever it is that you do to display that you're collaborative. This is your brand launch, so keep in mind how you want to be perceived and start sharing. We'll talk more about folding in your passions into your brand in chapter 6.

Growth: When a product is in the growth stage, it is quite popular. This is where it's selling the best, getting the most competitors, and hitting its stride in the market. The product is getting more distribution, getting more shelf space–everyone has one! This is the most thrilling time for any marketer as you watch your fledgling product start bringing in some serious profit. It's also an exciting time for your brand. This is where you'll see you're gaining your most social media followers. Perhaps you're getting retweeted or being friended on a regular basis? Perhaps you're getting frequent visits on your LinkedIn profile? Recruiters might now start writing to you about opportunities. Make sure you're spending this time building a presence for yourself. If you've primarily concentrated on one social medium, now might be the time to expand to another one. This is the time to make sure you're refining your brand, your unique perspective, and differentiating yourself from the competition. Anything is possible. The sky's the limit, so keep aiming for way beyond Mars! (I used to say the moon, but Mars is now far more popular.)

Maturity: The maturity phase of the product lifecycle is one of the most interesting and challenging. This is when your product typically plateaus. It's not growing or expanding. It may have saturated the market. It's possible that because of the popularity of the product in a given category it has many competitors. This is when you'll see "knock-offs" of a particular product start to crop up. For your brand, the maturity cycle might be the stage where you're a well-established expert in your field. You probably have a nice following on social media. You might have a position of leadership. You may be yielding bigger and more challenging projects. The key in the maturity cycle is to keep growing and bringing value. Challenge yourself to think differently about your brand and what you want your next stage in your career to embody.

Decline: When a product hits this stage in its life cycle, we start to see a slump in sales. There's either no longer a need for the product or service, or the cheaper "knockoffs" you saw emerge during the maturity phase have successfully taken over in market share. If you're in the decline part of your career, you might find yourself either retiring, or struggling to be relevant, or seeing a limited number of opportunities coming your way. Don't lose faith if you find yourself at this stage. This is when any good product manager starts to reassess features and functions and creates the next iteration of whatever it is, and if done properly, re-launches the product life cycle all over again. You can do the same for your personal brand. For you, it might be time to take stock of what you were known for during your maturity phase and regroup. There could be a new career for you out there with a few tweaks to your personal brand. The wonderful thing about the decline phase is the opportunity to relaunch yourself and your career and the entire cycle over again. You get to start at the beginning again with the "introduction" phase and watch your brand grow all over again.

Take a moment to determine where you are currently in your brand life cycle. It could be possible that you had a good position and a good career, but no one outside of your circle of colleagues knows much about you. And you may ask, why should they? This is where people argue with me, that it's all about knowing the right people. By building your brand and extending your reach, more of the right people *will* get to know you. Think of a great product that is sold only in a local store. Everyone in the town knows that by going to that mom-and-pop shop, you can get the most amazing "thing," but what happens if the mom-and-pop owners decide they want to sell the shop? Or retire? What if the only people who know about that amazing "thing" are a small group of people who decide to retire to Florida and not spread the word (if you're already retired in Florida, pretend you're not) to potential buyers? By keeping you and yourself the elite's best secret, you're doing yourself and your career a disservice. So, I say go ahead and let the world know the incredibly talented and value you are.

> Go ahead and let the world know the incredibly talented and value you are.

Personal Story: The Power of Reinvention

When I started my career, an incredible female executive called me into her office one day and told me she saw a lot of herself in me. She said I could have a great career, but she wanted to give me some advice. It was this: Get your MBA. (Short pause, I know some of you may not agree with her advice but read on anyway.)

At that point, I was barely out of college. I managed to get a job in an in-house advertising department of a video game company. I tried my hand at the agency world, and it wasn't for me. My goal was to eventually be promoted, so I could work on the commercials and go to live shoots. That was going to be fun! I wasn't even thinking about my long-term career.

"Why?" I asked her. I wasn't opposed to higher education, but I had just started paying back my undergraduate loans. Taking on additional debt wasn't part of the equation.

She explained it to me this way. She said, if I ever decided to get married and have a family and drop out of my career, my MBA will be a ticket back in. It would level the field so that when I went back into the job market and started interviewing, I wouldn't hear how I'd been out of the market too long and I needed to restart by answering phones. That degree would allow me to maintain a certain level upon reentry.

I thought about it. Two years later I left and joined the Fortune 50 where I spent a good portion of my career for one reason only—they would pay for my MBA. I added another level of growth to my personal brand with that degree. I was now invited to take a seat at a different table. That executive was one hundred percent correct in my case. An MBA was my entry ticket into many different roles and opportunities, and it has served me well.

Grow with It

Guest Column by Daphne J. Vought

Does thinking of yourself as a product seem impersonal or perhaps something reserved only for those with celebrity or influencer status? If so, I understand. I used to have those same thoughts and ideas. How could I be a "product?" Turns out, my brand is all about exploration and evolution! As we go through life, we can also choose to grow through life.

There's an expression, "you're either growing or shrinking, there is no maintaining." It's an accurate way to consider the advantages of progression and expansion in relation to our image, skills, and abilities.

Using the cliche of caterpillar to butterfly transformation, we can understand the benefit to growth. The progression from easily squashed creepy crawly to beautiful soaring creation is not limited to insects. As we transform, we also grow and mature.

The good news is no matter where you are on your journey, if you're still breathing there's still potential in you. What may seem like a decline in your current status or station can genuinely set you up for the greatest opportunity you can imagine.

> What may seem like a decline in your current status or station can genuinely set you up for the greatest opportunity you can imagine.

When you decide to take ownership of your possibilities and marketability, you take control of your potential. Everything in life is cyclical. What stage are you in currently? Will you choose to grow through it or stall out? It's up to you.

About the Contributor

Daphne J. Vought is a sought-after speaker, consultant, retreat facilitator, coach, and author. Daphne is passionate about empowering and equipping others to live by design instead of default. Accomplished in direct sales, corporate America, and vocational ministry, she now uses her experience and expertise to help other women recall, reclaim, and reach their dreams, dignity, and destiny.

Try It Out!

Take a moment to reflect where you think you are in your brand lifecycle and list it below. What challenges or benefits are you experiencing? What can you do to optimize this stage?

_____

_____

_____

_____

_____

Looking back at the social media vehicles you selected and what personal brand attributes you want to highlight, think through how you'll start engaging on those platforms. List a few ways you will start to engage differently.

1. _____

2. _____

3. _____

4. _____

5. _____

What you have learned in this chapter:

✓ Where you are in your brand life cycle.

✓ What actions you need to take to optimize your stage.

✓ How your chosen social media outlets will serve you in your current brand life cycle.

CHAPTER 6

Folding in Your Passions

At this point, I want to pause and congratulate you on what you have accomplished. Let's celebrate your wins.

- You have an "I am" statement.
- You know what qualities you want to demonstrate as your brand.
- You know your strengths.
- You've determined where you are in your brand cycle.

This might not seem like much, but it is. Up until now, it's probably more than you've thought about when it comes to your personal brand.

Now, let's talk a bit about your passions and how to fold them into your brand. *My passions?* you might ask. Yes! What is the first thing you think about when you wake up in the morning? Do you love running? What hobbies do you enjoy? Do you paint? Are you a poet? It doesn't matter one bit if you're good at any of these things. An archeologist once told Kurt Vonnegut, "I don't think doing a thing is the point of doing them. I think you've got all these wonderful experiences with different skills, and that all teaches you things and makes you an interesting person, no matter how well you do them."

All those wonderful hobbies, interests, and passions make you an interesting person. They help add depth to your personal brand. Think of them as salt (or insert favorite spice here if you're avoiding salt) to bring out the flavor of the special recipe that is you. By folding in your passions, they become another part of the "tree" that is you. Remember the tree from chapter 1? For our purposes, let's call your passion, hobbies, and interests the branches.

You might be thinking that you don't have any hobbies or passions or interests. You do, and here's how to figure them out. What are your favorite movies? What television series do you stream? What books do you read? If you don't have time to read, what would you like to read? Do you like the arts? What are your favorite museums? Do you spend your weekends taking amateur photos with your cellphone? Are you a massive fan of eating out? Do you have a favorite cuisine or restaurant? If you can answer these questions, you have passions!

And now I want to show you how to highlight these passions to illustrate the core elements of your personal brand. Let's say your "I am" statement describes you as a "creative problem-solver." When folding your passions into your brand, it would be completely appropriate to emphasize your love for art museums and the works of Van Gogh. (I'm a John William Waterhouse fan, myself.) Do you see how these interests demonstrate your creativity? Perhaps your "I am" statement indicates that you're a "collaborator" or "leader." An example of a well-matched passion might be coaching your son's soccer team. These connections might seem obvious, but it's always fascinating to me how often people omit their passions from their personal brand. As Vonnegut learned, these activities make us more interesting people and help others connect with us on a deeper level. As you build your personal brand presence, these "branches" of your tree can help differentiate you from others and attract people with like interests, which only increases your chances of reaching potential employers and clients and partners. People tend to gravitate to people who are like themselves.

Humans are complex. Not everything we like to do will fit perfectly into our personal branding statement. There might be hobbies or passions that you simply don't want to share with the rest of the world. That's perfectly reasonable. The key is being intentional and thoughtful about what you do share.

Go back to chapter 4 and look at the three social vehicles that you decided to use to communicate your personal brand. How can you start to infuse your passions and hobbies into your social media outlets? Is it a picture of your favorite Van Gogh painting that talks about how it relates to your brand attributes? Maybe you post something like this: "One way to increase your creative problem-solving skills is to think of things from a different perspective. Here's one of my favorite paintings and museums to visit when I have to think through a challenging issue." See what those two sentences just did? It made your brand attribute of "creative problem-solver" concrete. Somewhere someone scrolled through a feed, stopped at your post, read it, and started to form an opinion about you and your skill set on a subconscious level. If you're lucky, you might have even gained an authentic follower.

What about the soccer coach? Everyone loves to talk about winning, but what about a photo of your team in a huddle before the game and a post that said, "Today, the soccer team I coach lost. They played a good game, but we just couldn't pull through. The best part? We held our heads high, shook hands with the opposing players, and learned what we must do better. That was a gift." That post brings out the attributes

> The key is being intentional and thoughtful about what you do share.

of collaboration and leadership and helps others draw positive conclusions about the leadership qualities of the person posting. He handles defeat with grace and sportsmanship, he leads by example, and he learns from his mistakes. He demonstrates collaboration by congratulating the other team, by implying his team will improve, learns from the defeat, and views it in a positive light. I'm sure you might see other qualities in the post that I haven't listed. I don't know about you, but his attitude is one that resonates with me. He would be a person I would like to have on my team, which is the entire point of building your personal brand.

I do want to take a moment to offer a word of caution. Religion has been and always will be a hot topic of discussion and might or might not be appropriate to your brand. If you're a youth pastor or religion teacher, discussing religion and your perspective will be an attribute to your brand. If you're not, carefully consider what you're willing to share with the world and the way you're willing to share it. Many larger corporations adopt an agnostic perspective, dictating that employees avoid religious discussion in professional settings. Another sensitive topic is political affiliation or special interest groups. If this is part of your professional job function, you'll likely talk about them, but if not, I would again recommend caution in a professional setting. Whether you work for a federal, state, or local government agency in the United States or a private employer, it's important to use caution when expressing political views online. Much of what we say is certainly protected under the First Amendment, but private companies, in particular, are within their rights to set limits. Remember that everything you post online might potentially exist forever, even if you delete it.

You can now take your "I am" statement and add some color to it. For me, it might read, "I am an innovative, enthusiastic, and collaborative marketing strategist and storyteller who is an award-winning poet and bestselling author who believes in the power of stories."

Personal Story: Be Your Authentic Self

I hear a voice in the back of my mind when I know I'm going to embark on something scary. It belongs to a former boss of mine who once told me, "You are a horrible writer. You are absolutely awful. You really should never write." Needless to say, we don't speak—like ever.

Here's the thing—I love writing. On any given day, I spend most of my time writing–even if it's emails. It makes me happy. My poetry book won three awards. My work of fiction debuted as a #1 new release and #1 bestseller on Amazon, earned many positive reviews, and recently won an award. Woo-hoo!

For the longest time, however, I hid my love for writing. I was afraid I would be ridiculed again. It hurts deeply when people belittle the things you love or pass judgement on things you aspire to be. I hid my authentic self, burying it deep. I never raised my hand for storytelling assignments or anything where I would need to write. I didn't even tell my colleagues I had launched a poetry book. *Would they read it and hate it? Would they make fun of me? Would they say the same thing my jerk boss said?* Eventually I took a deep breath and started to share my work with a few people, and an amazing thing happened. I found others at work who loved what I loved. They also wrote stories, novels, and poetry. They too had a passion and a dream. They too found joy in writing.

> I encourage you to step into your authentic self and fully embrace your passions.

When my fictional work was launched, my employer published an internal article about it and featured it around the globe. They even threw me a little party. Those actions warmed my heart.

I encourage you to step into your authentic self and fully embrace your passions. You'll find that other people share them, and no longer will you feel alone. In sharing them, you'll give other people permission to share also, so they won't feel alone. Nothing squelches a nay-sayer faster than living your true, passionate life.

Clarify What Matters Most

Guest Colum by María Tomás-Keegan

Having thirty years of corporate leadership experience and reinventing myself multiple times, I discovered how essential it became to fold passions into my brand and work, especially as I became an entrepreneur. It was the key to becoming satisfied, happy, and in harmony with life. It's a lofty goal—and achievable when you are intentional and persistent.

As Valerie says, not all passions are created equal. That means some will align with the work you do in the world and some won't. They are all a part of who you are, and knowing who you are is the foundation upon which you build your personal brand. No excuses. No hiding. It's about you being you.

The exercises and examples in this chapter will help you clarify what matters most to you, what lights you up, and how you might turn your passion into a profession—whether you work for a corporation or for yourself. That's what I did when I left the corporate world.

I followed my passion for helping others make conscious and confident career choices based on who they are and what they want in life. I teach them how to turn their vision into reality. Knowing what you're passionate about is a big part of the formula.

You might think this isn't so important and that you can skip over the passion part of personal branding. But before you do, you might want to ask yourself these questions:

- How much better would my work and life be if I were motivated to jump out of bed every morning, raring to go?

- What would it feel like to love where I work, who I work with, and being able to make a difference?

- Who else in my world could I positively impact when I am happy and satisfied with who I am and what I'm doing?

If you came up with some serious answers, there are no shortcuts, and folding in your passions will make the work you're doing worthwhile and exceptionally satisfying. Take it from me!

About the Contributor

María Tomás-Keegan is a multi-certified career and life coach specializing in helping women turn career and life transitions into personal triumphs! She creatively blends her 30-year corporate leadership experience and training with the lessons learned from navigating life-changing events like loss, divorce, and career upheavals. María has been called a master of reinvention and is passionate about coaching and mentoring women who struggle to find meaning and purpose in their careers and life—bringing a calm force into what can feel like chaos. María partners with women to create a firm foundation for confidently leaping into their next chapter while gathering life-long tools to help them thrive. María is also an award-winning author and speaker and hosts the weekly international broadcast called *Tips for the Transition: The Career Roadmap.*

Try It Out!

List five things you consider your passions or hobbies in the space below. If you have more, keep going! My passions and hobbies are:

1. _____
2. _____
3. _____
4. _____
5. _____

Look at your five hobbies and passions and line them up to the adjectives you used to build your "I am" statement. You can write your "I am" statement in the space below if it helps you complete the exercise.

Passion/Hobby	Adjective that aligns to in your "I am" statement

_____

_____

_____

_____

_____

What you have learned in this chapter:

✓ Your list of passions.

✓ How your passions help augment your personal brand and add "flavor" and "depth."

✓ How to infuse your passions into your social media.

✓ A revised "I am" statement to use as your guide.

CHAPTER 7

Building Your Personal Narrative

One of the exciting things about the work you've done so far is being able to get a renewed perspective on who you are and what you have to offer. Now it's time to put it all together into a personal narrative that will help you further define and articulate your personal brand. You can use this narrative in a variety of ways. It can serve as a two-minute elevator pitch, a LinkedIn profile summary, a resume summary, or a biography. Let's look more closely at each of these tools.

Two-Minute Elevator Pitch

Anyone who's experienced the situation of unemployment and an outplacement talent agency will be familiar with the two-minute elevator pitch. It's essentially a quick summary about you and your skills. It can also be edited down to a thirty-second pitch or some derivation thereof. The goal is to give a prospective interviewer an idea of who you are, why they want to keep talking to you, and how you are exactly what they need. The elevator pitch essentially becomes the commercial for brand YOU. A quick search on Google will tell you the fundamental elements of a two-minute elevator pitch with a variety of small tweaks depending on the source. The University of North Texas Health Sciences department provides these guidelines:

- Personal and Education (15 seconds)
- Early Career/Life Experiences (15-30 seconds)
- Recent Work History/Life Experiences (45-60 seconds)
- Why you are here (15-30 seconds)

Here's an example of an elevator pitch.

I have a degree in finance, and I will be graduating this December. While attending college, I was able to work 20 hours each week interning for XYZ financial institution in both my senior and junior years. I was able to get real-life experience in experience in cost accounting, cash-flow analysis, and budget development, and assisted in preparing client proposals. In addition, I've continued to expand by technical skills and am proficient in ABC programs. I'm excited to have a future career in banking. My ultimate goal is to become a loan officer so I can help people secure better futures and outcomes for themselves. Would it be possible for me to schedule a few minutes to learn how you were able to achieve your position? I would welcome your advice.

The graphic below gives you an easy-to-remember version.

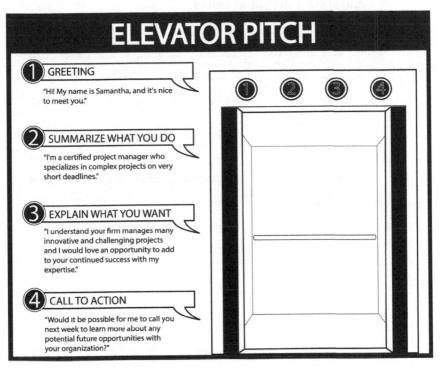

Redesigned from https://www.indeed.com/career-advice/interviewing/
how-to-give-an-elevator-pitch-examples

Use the following spaces to start building out your elevator pitch with the break down described above.

1. Introduce yourself. Include your education.

_____

_____

_____

_____

_____

2. Provide a summary of what you do. Include relevant career information here. You can also reference why chose your potential career.

   _____

   _____

   _____

   _____

   _____

3. Explain what you want. You can include relevant facts on how you can help whatever organization or person you're pitching.

   _____

   _____

   _____

   _____

   _____

4. Ask for what you want and summarize your selling point.

   _____

   _____

   _____

   _____

   _____

LinkedIn Profile Summary

LinkedIn is a professional networking site with approximately 875 million users and over 58 million registered companies. If you're a professional and not on LinkedIn, you probably should be. Your LinkedIn profile summary is an overview of your personal brand narrative found in the "About" section. This is where potential employers and recruiters go to learn more about you. The first few sentences in the about section are critical because they carry an above-the-fold meaning. They are what someone looking at your profile will read before they have to click "read more" and unfold the page. You'll use this space to succinctly describe who you are, what you do, the value you offer, and any awards and recognition you might have received in the past.

Here's an example:

About:

I am an innovative and strategic marketing communications manager adept at campaign management, content creation, and message development across multiple digital and traditional marketing channels. I've won several awards for outstanding marketing campaign performance. In addition, I have a strong ability to drive teams through collaboration with specific focus in agile marketing techniques to help teams exceed expectations. I have a deep passion for the art and craft of marketing.

My specific industry expertise includes retail, telecommunications, and media and entertainment.

When I'm not working, you'll find me exploring the world, one bike ride at a time.

Resume Summary

Most resumes have a space to highlight a summary of experiences or an objective. Many include phrases such as "to use my skills to provide value" or "to join a fast-growing company and expand my skill set." You get the idea. The bottom line is you are applying because you want a particular job. The goal is to grab attention and get the interview.

Here's an example:

Accomplished and results-driven Marketing & Communications Leader with broad based expertise leading the development of innovative and effective strategies and campaigns that drive the success of companies, brands, and people in highly competitive markets.

Ability to collaborate with key stakeholders to structure and execute corporate communications strategies that foster increased engagement and visibility.

An enthusiastic and effective leader who leverages true passion and unwavering commitment to excellence to direct high-visibility marketing initiatives. A demonstrated record of success and achievement marked by a series of promotions to positions of increased influence, authority, and accountability.

> "Val is a tremendous asset to our team. Val is committed to continuous learning, which allows her to make contributions outside her day-to-day responsibility. Val can take a vague request, define it, and execute a good outcome."
> –Glenn D. Former
> C-Suite Executive

Your Narrative as a Story

While we've talked about elevator pitches and examples of how to highlight your value as a professional, I want to take a side-step here and talk about the power of your narrative. And, if you'll indulge me, I'm going to change the word "narrative" to "story."

First, let me define what I mean by story. For me, a story doesn't describe who, what, when, where, and how. A story, in my world, is something far more precious. It's bound together gently with the word "why." Of all the people in all the world wanting whatever it is you want, why you? (The alternative and probably more powerful question is why not you? But that's an entirely different book.)

The most powerful way to answer the "why you" question is through a story. A story has a beginning that sets the scene, a middle that includes some form of conflict, and an end that resolves the conflict and serves as a conclusion. A compelling story also allows the listener or reader to see, feel, smell, and imagine what happens. It allows the listener or reader to emotionally invest in what's happening and in the outcome. Ever read a book and just lose the entire day? Ever watch a movie and wonder where in the world the two or three hours of the day went? That's the power of story. A good story can be transformative. It can change how you look at the world and how you will interact with it in the future. A good story can shift your thinking, and as a result, your actions. A good story is magic created by humans to celebrate our common experience.

Researchers have identified neurological aspects to storytelling. In short, when you tell a story, the

> Our brains are *wired* to tell and hear stories.

part of your brain that activates to remember the story is also activated in the listener. Our brains are *wired* to tell and hear stories. Stories helps us remember facts and figures. Stories help us make decisions. Stories help us interpret and connect with the world around us. All of which makes storytelling an extremely powerful tool in any form of brand building.

Why am I taking you through a quick overview of stories? Because how you tell your story is important. The story of you. All the chapters prior to this point have focused on the adjectives that describe you. The value you bring. Your "I am" statement. What social media platforms to utilize and for what part of your personal brand. And even how to use your passions to "flavor" your brand. Now, it's time for you to tell your story!

Personal Story: There's Always Hope

When I was in elementary school, I was a terrible student. During parent-teacher nights, teachers often told my mother there was little hope for me achieving any notable academic success. My standardized test scores were low. To top it off, I lived in a welfare building in the wrong part of town, which compounded the teachers' negative assumptions about my destiny.

My education continued in that manner until the fifth grade when I encountered a teacher unlike any other. This teacher was resilient, and she saw something in me that no one else saw. She made it clear I would not be a failure in her class. I was going to work hard. Before I knew it, my desk was set next to hers. I spent my lunches working in her classroom. Whenever I got anything wrong, I heard her brassy voice announcing my error to the class. "Come on, honey!" I cried every day. Every. Single. Day.

Then an amazing thing happened. I got my first grade of one hundred on an assignment. I remember holding that paper in my hand and looking it over several times to make sure it was mine. Yes. That was my handwriting. Yes. That was my name. Yes. That was my test. That was my grade. An A-plus. One hundred percent. I cried, but this time for a different reason. I was overwhelmed with an incredible sense of joy. It was the first of many A-pluses to pepper my academic career. I went on to graduate high school at the top of my class, attend college on scholarships, and have my employer pay for my MBA. Amazing things happened because someone believed in me. At ten years old. At whatever age you are right now, you shouldn't back away either.

Tell Your Story

Guest Column by Louis Richardson

I've been blessed to have met and worked alongside thousands of people during my career. And as I reflect, the faces that rise above the rest are the characters who have shared stories of their journey, and in doing so, earned a place in my memory. As someone interested in improving your personal brand and narrative, you should consider investing time and thought in your story.

I often told my sales teams their message should not be about what the product or service does, but rather what people can do because the product or service exists. Similarly, when you consider your story, think less about what you do or have done, and share what that means to others.

While coaching a diverse audience of sales professionals, I challenged them with this idea and asked them to share their purpose in six words or less. When asked, one gentleman responded, "I keep the monsters away." That answer piqued my curiosity, and I asked him to tell me more. He shared he was in the business of doing corporate background checks that provided his customers the security in knowing they didn't have monsters lurking in their organizations. Of the dozens of answers that day, I remember that one.

Carefully designing your story and making it relative to your listener's story is one of the most effective ways of connecting your brand and message to your listener's journey.

For more than a decade, I served as chief storyteller for IBM Watson Work and Talent. I was often asked, "What does a Chief Storyteller do?" That was my invitation to briefly share my story and relevance. Since you might be asking the same question, here is an example of my reply, "I assist in moving people along a journey of belief." That, in turn, would spark a request for clarification or example. At this point, the listener is not only paying attention but also expressing interest and desire for more conversation. I would unfold the next layer of my story, guiding them into their discovery of the relevance of our conversation to their journey. Remember, people are naturally curious, so use that as you tell your story.

Carefully designing your story and making it relative to your listener's story is one of the most effective ways of connecting your brand and message to your listener's journey.

About the Contributor

Louis Richardson, chief storyteller and corporate story coach, has served as the chief storyteller for a Fortune 50 and has appeared on numerous stages and interviews about the power of storytelling, including *Adweek*. He has developed educational certifications for storytellers, as well as empowered executive leaders in the Fortune 500 to embrace the belief that stories matter.

Try It Out!

Think back to the personal story I shared in this chapter. What did you learn about me? What adjectives would you use to describe me? Will you remember my story? If so, what parts?

_____

_____

_____

_____

_____

Now it's your turn. Select an adjective from those that make up your "I am" statement and think of a "story" that tells someone how you have demonstrated that adjective. Write it in the space below. Then write your story so it has a beginning, middle, and end. Make sure to make it descriptive so someone can imagine what you saw and how you felt.

Adjective	Personal Story
	Beginning Middle End
	Beginning Middle End

	Beginning
	Middle
	End

Do you have a great example of what you do like in Louis's story? List your ideas below.

_____

_____

_____

_____

_____

What you have learned in this chapter:

- ✓ The definition of an elevator pitch and how to give one.
- ✓ What to include in your resume and LinkedIn profile.
- ✓ The definition of story.
- ✓ The importance of story to your narrative.
- ✓ Stories you can use to illustrate your personal brand.

CHAPTER 8

What Are You Wearing?

Lately, there's been a lot of talk about "bringing your whole self to work" and "being your whole self." I'm here to tell you, honestly, no one wants to know your whole self at work. Not. One. Human. Being. Take a moment. Read that again. No one wants to know your whole self at work. There. I repeated it. Here's to it sticking.

The people who do want to know your whole self are your family, friends, and significant others. Your work colleagues? Absolutely not. But wait, you might say, "We just spent six chapters talking about how unique and impressive I am. We discussed my attributes, hobbies, and passions. I'm so interesting! And now you're saying don't bring my whole self to work?" Yup! Here's why. You'll note in your exercises you had to cross things out. You had to discern which attributes, hobbies, and passions aligned with your personal brand. You had to determine which "branches" of your tree you wanted to share with the professional world at large.

We are simply continuing that approach. No one wants to see your "whole self" in sweatpants, sweatshirts, or any form of athletic wear unless that's your uniform because you work at a gym. Shakespeare wrote in Act II, Scene VII of the play *As You Like It*, "All the world's a stage, And all the men and women merely players." Brilliant. So, if the world is indeed a stage, what's your costume? In other words, what are you wearing?

I can still hear some of you objecting to this idea. Perhaps you feel that you should be comfortable. Does it really matter if you're wearing yoga pants under your suit jacket? People are supposed to judge you by what you say and do and not what you wear, right? Yes. Absolutely one hundred percent true unless they're paying you to show up. The fundamental difference between the coffee-stained blue T-shirt you wear when watching the Sunday game on your couch and the ironed, buttoned-up dress shirt you wear to work on Monday morning is simple. On Monday morning you're on company time, and someone is going to write you a check at the end of the week. On Sunday, you're on your own time. No one's paying you. Spill and wear coffee at your leisure. What if you have a uniform that you wear to work? Great question. Simple answer—keep it clean, ironed, and repaired.

> The fundamental difference between the coffee-stained blue T-shirt you wear when watching the Sunday game on your couch and the ironed, buttoned-up dress shirt you wear to work on Monday morning is simple. On Monday morning, you're on company time.

How you show up and the costume you're wearing when people pay you, speaks volumes about your personal brand. The amount of time you spend brushing your teeth, brushing your hair, and keeping your clothes clean, tidy, and ironed, lets your employers know you're serious about the work you perform for them and any clients you might encounter.

What to consider when getting dressed for work:

- Does it fit properly? Or is it too oversized or too tight?

- Is it the right length? In the sleeves, pant legs, skirt lengths?
- Is the pattern distracting?
- Are the colors coordinated and not distracting?
- Are you wearing the right shoes?

I want to take a moment and talk about the often-forgotten element of shoes. They absolutely do not need to be expensive. But they do need to be clean and, if applicable, polished.

A quick Google search will give you an idea of what not to wear to work, but here are a few things I recommend avoiding:

- ripped jeans of any form and possibly jeans all together
- stretched fabric or "athletic" pants, leggings, or yoga pants that pretend to be tailored (unless part of your uniform)
- tank tops, halter tops, and sleeveless shirts
- anything see-through or can pass for lingerie
- pajamas in any form
- T-shirts, especially ones with offensive or divisive phrases or images
- flip flops, beachy slides, or plastic footwear (unless a podiatrist told you this was the only footwear you can wear)
- sweatshirts or hoodies
- anything with a stain on it
- baseball caps (unless part of a uniform)

If you're still confused whether something would be work appropriate, you can search online retailers of all price points and look for their "wear to work" or "office attire." Most have a section that will fit those criteria. I'm not saying you must wear suits every day or designer clothing. But you do need to take care with your appearance. What you're wearing will tell people volumes about your personal brand. You want to make sure you're putting your best impression forward. As much as we'd like to think that people don't judge us based on our appearance, research continues to show that this happens frequently. In fact, *Princeton Research* indicated that people judge your competence based on your clothes in under one second. If nothing else, get yourself a full-length mirror (IKEA® has some inexpensive ones) and take a good look at yourself before you go to work.

Sometimes people decide that a certain attire will become part of their personal brand. Maybe it's a color? A piece of jewelry? A type of shoe? If you do decide to go with a "gimmick," make sure that it's sustainable as styles change and it's representative of your overall brand or purpose. For example, if you always wear yellow because it's your favorite color, your brand attribute is "cheerful" and color theory confirms that yellow is often associated with pleasant and optimistic feelings, then go for it. If you're still not convinced, I'd like to direct you to any episode of *What Not to Wear*, a popular TV series from 2003-2013. The lessons on that popular television show still apply.

Wardrobe Tips

Article of clothing	Where it should fall
Pant legs for men	¼ inch off the floor
Shirt sleeves for men	They should come to then base of your hand with a ¼ to a ½ inch shown when wore under a suit jacket.
Shirt jackets and sports coats for men	Determine the distance between the base of your neck and the ground and have the end of your suit jacket fall half the distance. Suit jackets and sports coats should have sleeves fall between ¼ and ¾ of an inch about base of your hand to allow for the shirt sleeves under it to show.
Skirts and dresses for women	Not shorter than two inches above your knee. Also, not long enough so you trip on it when walking.

Personal Story: Mind Your Seams

I had the unique opportunity to attend a session where a powerful female CMO took to stage to talk about the incredible things the business was doing under her direction. I remember sitting in the back row, just staring. Her A-line skirt was on wrong. Somehow the seams had shifted and instead of falling nicely and moving with her, she looked like she had a stiff cone-shaped thing around her body. It looked as if she were acting in a bad stage play wearing a bad stage costume.

Now before you get all hostile and ask me why I'm so judgy about her attire, I want you to consider that she represented a multi-billion-dollar business, made an incredible living, and was there to gain the confidence of other high-level executives so that they would sign multi-million-dollar deals. She represented me, my profession, and the company I worked for. That was her role. The least she could do was look in the mirror or ask one of her "handlers" this simple question, "How do I look?"

What struck me was that no one saw fit to make sure that, before she got on that stage, she looked good. That signaled for me one of two things: she wasn't a person to pay attention to details, or no one on her staff either liked her or cared enough to make her look good. (For reference, wherever possible, I always made sure every one of my executives looks amazing on camera, in pictures, and on stage. I love my executives.)

After the event, when everyone cleared out, I fumbled with my bags to hear the debrief with her team. Suffice it to say that one of the two assumptions I made above was correct. How you dress says more about you than you think.

It's Okay to Dress for Effect

Guest Column by Jessica White

Business on the top. Yoga on the bottom. That's become the new wardrobe of the web conference era. But soon, and hopefully sooner rather than later, we will be back to connecting face to face. For that return, we will need to refresh ourselves on the importance of how we dress. The old adage of first impressions will again be our reality.

Traditionally, we think of clothes as form and function. They keep us warm or protect us from the elements. In history, clothing was leveraged to display wealth and status. But, clothes, much like our words and our body language, can be used as a tool to drive outcomes when used intentionally.

What we wear changes the way people interact with us, and it changes our relationship to them. We can dress for effect.

Early in my career, in the era before employee experience was a corporate initiative, I had the fortunate or unfortunate experience of learning how to leverage tools like appearance to change my reality.

I had an executive who was a bully. He was worse than a bully. He randomly selected people in the organization to metaphorically "break," then he would hold up their failed achievements as an example of where he found a hole and fixed it. For some reason, I was next on the list.

For visual reference, this man was six foot five and had an intimidating ogre-like presence. For where I was in my career, I was at the top of my game but low in the pecking order. I was determined not to let this guy take me down. I had my act together, but it seemed no amount of convincing was going to change his course.

A female executive who was his direct report took me aside. She had had a similar experience. She had dressed for impact and had come out on tom. She suggested I do the same.

I am a tall woman, but the day of our next meeting, I was the tallest. I wore stilettos and an all-black, very structured suit. I felt confident and powerful. When he stepped into the room, I stood up. I was eye to eye with him. I leaned in, and he seemed to mentally stumble back. He stopped being my bully.

Christian Louboutin said, "Shoes transform your body language and attitude. They lift you physically and emotionally." That day I was lifted up.

> "Shoes transform your body language and attitude. They lift you physically and emotionally."
> –Christian Louboutin

Clothing can be a powerful asset. Colors, textures, shape—all these things invoke feelings, memories. They communicate a lot of information about the wearer, and they elicit behavior from observers.

Scientists Hajo Adam and Adam D. Galinsky conducted an experiment in 2012, and the notion of "enclothed cognition" was born. Enclothed cognition is defined as the effect that clothing has upon a person's mental process and the way they think, feel, and function in areas like attention, confidence, or abstract thinking.

Clothing can be a self-defense weapon, it can be a white flag, it can be a token of friendship and a way of reaching across the aisle.

In this case, the dark color and a structured suit conveyed confidence, resolution, something formidable, power. Tall shoes conveyed confidence.

There are so many ways to leverage clothing, shoes, and accessories to get a desired effect. Bright colors invoke creativity and energy. Leveraged in a team breakout for ideation, they can be effective for encouraging out-of-the-box thinking, and they can help your colleagues see you in a different light. Bright colors are also proven to lift your spirits.

The color red and pointed shoes symbolize focus and a desire to get things done.

Cotton, muslin, and light colors convey relatability, approachability, friendliness, and are non-threatening. I use these colors and fabrics when I want to connect. This is ideal if you are joining a team and want to exude a non-threatening vibe or want to be accepted in a new group at work.

The power in being intentional about what you wear is not just about influencing and taking an active role in how people perceive you, but it changes how you feel about you... and that in itself is persuasive.

Edith Head, a heavily awarded costume designer from the mid-1900s, said it best, "You can have anything you want in life if you dress for it." What will you wear today?

About the Contributor

Jessica White is a growth leader and creative strategist with a history of bringing complementary technologies together from some of the world's biggest companies, companies like NASCAR®, The Weather Company, Salesforce, Google, Microsoft®, and IBM. She thrives on seeing new businesses come to light and is known in the tech industry for taking practices to their next level of growth. Jessica is a working mother, and together with her husband, she is very active in the Christian community and the arts. She has a passion for constructs, which create an understanding of people and their talents, and strives to be in service to others. As a career coach, Jessica helps connect people through their strengths to fulfilling career paths.

Try It Out!

Go into your closet and find something that makes you feel amazing and try it on.

Write down all the emotions you're feeling and see how you are holding yourself in the mirror.

_____

_____

_____

_____

_____

Are there articles of clothing that don't fit well, but you keep them anyway? Pull those pieces out and donate them.

What are you wearing to work now? If you need to change your wardrobe, what will you change?

_____

_____

_____

_____

_____

What you have learned from this chapter:

✓ Align your work attire with your personal brand.

✓ Make sure your clothing fits well and is appropriate.

✓ Coordinate your shoes to your attire.

CHAPTER 9

Ready for Your Close Up

In the new world we live in, most business is now conducted via video instead of in person. My guess is that most of your meetings are either on Zoom™, Webex®, Microsoft Teams®, Google Meet™, or a similar virtual meeting platform. While I prefer this mode of communication, there are many professionals who are still mourning the loss of frequent air travel, face-to-face meetings, and a good firm handshake.

While we're living in this new virtual work reality, it's time to show up for the camera looking your very best. We already talked about what you should be wearing in chapter 8, and although I know most people say it doesn't matter what you're wearing on your bottom half—assuming the camera lens cuts you off mid-waist—I would still be mindful. You never know when you might accidentally spill that hot cup of coffee while moving your arm and stand up in shock. Just saying.

Zoom offers a "touch up my appearance" option. Select your menu settings and then select "video" settings. This option smooths out any obvious blemishes or marks and adds an extra layer of polish to your appearance.

Backgrounds

Most virtual video platforms allow you to add a virtual background. You can find several of these on sites like Pixabay and Unsplash. You can also make your own in Photoshop, Canva, or other software tools. Your company or organization might also have a background that they've developed for employee use.

If you're not able to use a virtual background, or the idea that you might disappear if you move your arms or lean too far back in your chair frightens you, look at your environment. Make sure that there's nothing offensive behind you on a bookshelf, on a wall, or on a table (same with whatever mug you place within view of your camera.) Try to avoid anything that might look disheveled in your background like piles of papers, laundry, an unmade bed—you get the idea. If you're trying to decide where to set up in your home, you can't go wrong with a bare wall.

Lighting and Camera Angles

WikiHow offers three simple ways to look good on Zoom. Your primary light source should always be in front of you. If you can, turn your computer so you're facing a window instead of having the window behind you. Facing a window brings in a lot of light that will help you look natural on camera.

If you don't have a window, consider investing in a ring light that can be placed behind your computer or clamped on to your computer screen. If you can, also add a regular lamp from your home or a desk lamp behind your computer. If you can, manage two additional lights (maybe small ones scavenged from your home. My son's desk lamp is a personal favorite.) and place them at 10:00 and 2:00 angled toward your face—not behind your computer.

It's extremely important to position your camera at the right angle. You want to make sure you appear your very best and avoid any dark shadows that might fall on your face. To do this, line up the camera so it's at the same level as your eyes. You can put books, boxes, or anything else sturdy to raise the camera to make sure the lens is at the right angle.

Personal Story: What's That Behind You?

I don't know about you, but every time I'm in a virtual meeting, I stare at people's backgrounds. You can tell a lot about a person based on the surrounding artwork, books, and photographs. People give away a lot in their home environments. Even when people use a virtual background, I make a point of studying the one they selected. It can tell you a lot about their personality. There's a plethora of options, and I'm always intrigued by what people choose.

Due to my level of inquisitiveness and because I don't want others distracted like I can be, every time my business until holds an internal town hall, I make a point of developing a common corporate virtual background. Here are a few reasons why:

- It allows all the participants to feel as if we're in the same virtual space.
- It builds a sense of camaraderie.
- It provides an opportunity to highlight our company logo to remind everyone this is still work.
- It helps to elevate the conversation to the next level and prevent distractions.

Always Be Ready to Pivot

Guest Column by Shihan Mike Iannone

I am an enthusiastic 7th-degree black belt martial artist and shihan (teacher), fighter, and business owner. You can say that the martial arts are part of my DNA, and I take pride in helping my students unleash their potential. The motto at my school, Dragon Gate Martial Arts Academy, is simple: become your best self. It is something I truly believe in, and I want my students to believe too.

When the first wave of the pandemic hit, like many business owners, my wife and I were hit with a shutdown order. But my wife and I had worked too hard in our career and business to go down without a fight. While many of my counterparts could not figure out a way to teach martial arts in a non-physical environment, I pivoted. Like I tell my students, I decided to dedicate myself to learning a new approach and not letting myself give up. I was not going to go down. Instantaneously, I had to change my entire business model and go online. This wasn't something I ever imagined I would have to do. But I did it. I invested in Zoom, an online video conferencing platform that allowed me to teach live classes virtually. We also had to invest in internet cables, tablets, and a stand to hang from my ceiling.

At first, teaching virtually was hard. We had to decide whether students would turn their camera on so we can see them or have them leave it off.

We set up the camera so our logo was in the background. At first, we did this in our dining room. We took apart our dining room table and set a banner of our logo on the back wall. And placed mats on the floor. We wanted to make everyone feel as comfortable as possible and like they were still at the dojo training. It is very important to feel like you are a martial artist. When we were teaching, we still wore our

Karate uniforms in an effort to keep it very professional like we were still in our dojo.

The fire marshal for our town eventually gave us permission to teach in our dojo virtually. We had more room, better lighting, and I had everything where I needed it to teach the classes. But I still need to reconfigure the environment to provide the best experience for my students. I put tape on the mats, so I would know exactly where to stand to stay within the boundaries of the video. I wore a Blue Tooth headset to block out any other noise from entering the video. Finally, we made sure the students saw our main wall with our business logo, the American Flag, and the Martial Arts Creed. We felt this was important not only to make everyone feel comfortable, but to also hold us accountable to continuing to provide great service to every student who entered our school.

To keep the students engaged, we had to change the curriculum. We stopped teaching long forms with many moves and moving in all different directions. We did everything straight forward and made the combos shorter. We highlighted students when they were doing something great. We do this in our live classes when someone is trying hard.

We also played games. Sometimes I would make believe we were trying to hit them and when they saw it coming, they had to block and hit us back. This was a fun way to keep their eyes on the screen. They could not play the game if they were not paying attention. We also got the parents involved by holding pads, pillows, or even buying equipment their children could use at home.

Then we did some themed classes on May 4 called "May The 4th Be With You." We sent out a video earlier in the week of my wife making a lightsaber out of a pool noodle and some different colored tape we found at a craft store. We used our projector to shoot videos on a wall, so it looked as if they were in space, and we used our sound system to play Star Wars music. We taught our sword techniques with the lightsabers, which the students had made with their parents before the class.

My message here is this: never give up on yourself; never think something is impossible; always try your very best. It's amazing what you can accomplish in life if you are dedicated to your

> Never give up on yourself; never think something is impossible; always try your very best.

craft and willing to learn and listen to advice. My wife and I worked very hard to keep our school going. While I was teaching, she was looking at the screen to make sure everyone was keeping up, while taking care of our son and daughter. We did this for five months until we reopened again. And to this day, we are still running virtual classes through Zoom, even though we are open for in-person training.

About the Contributor

Shihan Mike Iannone has been training in martial arts since September 1990. He is a 7th Degree Black Belt in Kempo Tai-jitsu, 7th Degree Black Belt in Kempo Taekwondo, 1st Degree Black Belt in Modern Fa Rang Mu Sul. Iannone is trained in boxing, MMA, Jiu-jitsu, submission wrestling, Shotokan karate, and Tang Soo Do, as well as martial arts weapons bō staff, sword, stick, and short stick, and was a professional mixed martial arts fighter. He also taught for Ed Gross Karate Club From 1992 to 1999. Iannone has owned the Dragon Gate Martial Arts Academy since December 1999.

Try It Out!

Find your favorite spot in your house where you take your virtual meetings.

What's in your background?

- Is there something you can add to make it interesting? Maybe it's a plant. Or a photograph or a piece of art.
- Is there anything you should remove?
- Evaluate the lighting. See how it will look when you move the light sources around.

Show up on camera as your best self!

What you have learned in this chapter:

- ✓ Think about what your camera sees in your background.

- ✓ Remember to be conscious of what you're wearing (even below the camera lens).

- ✓ Note your lighting sources.

- ✓ Note where your camera is positioned.

CHAPTER 10

Next Steps

Congratulations! You made it through. By now you should have a clearer idea of what your personal brand is. This is important because—as I said at the beginning of this book—if you're not creating your personal brand, someone else is doing it for you. No one on the planet knows you better than you know yourself. Not even your mom.

Life is a glorious and tremendous adventure. I want you to use this book as a guide to help you imagine what you want next for your life. Every time you decide to reinvent yourself, pull out this book and go through the exercises. The average person will hold twelve different jobs in their lifetime and might even go on to have seven different careers. Given those averages, there are plenty of opportunities to try again.

You are a brilliant and wonderful work in progress. I have no doubt you were born to share your talents with the world. You might even develop new talents. Isn't that an exciting thing to ponder? Whatever shape your professional journey takes, I hope you enjoy it. Every one of us can provide value through the work we do, and our work will evolve as we evolve. Enjoy the process and adventure. Here's to the unleashing the power of you!

Try It Out!

- Embody your "I am" statement.

- Select your social media accounts and make sure the content you're posting is aligned with your personal brand traits. If it isn't, however tempting, don't post it. Remember: the internet is forever—at least for now.

- Embrace your passions and weave them into your personal brand. They will highlight your authenticity and your uniqueness. You are a combination of your passions, your personality, and your profession. They all come together to form your personal brand.

- Show up dressed properly. Enough said.

- Update your LinkedIn profile.

- Make sure virtual you is as well represented as in-person you.

- Dream, believe, and then achieve.

BIBLIOGRAPHY

Chapter 1

Branson, Richard. "Your brand name is only as good as your reputation." AZ Quotes. https://www.azquotes.com/quote/705729.

Lincoln, Abraham. "Character is like a tree and the reputation is like its shadow. The shadow is what we think of it; the tree is the real thing." Brainy Quotes. https://www.brainyquote.com/quotes/abraham_lincoln_121094.

Miko, I. "Mitosis, meiosis, and inheritance." *Nature Education* 1(2008): 206.

Robbins, Mel. "How to Stop Screwing Yourself." TEDxSF. https://youtu.be/Lp7E973zozc.

Smith, Drew. How Many Possible Combinations of DNA Are There? https://www.forbes.com/sites/quora/2017/01/20/how-many-possible-combinations-of-dna-are-there/?sh=751269355835.

Chapter 2

Wikipedia. "Branding." Updated May 27, 2022. https://en.wikipedia.org/wiki/Branding.

Chapter 4

Howarth, Josh. "Time Spent Using Smartphones (2022 Statistics)." *Exploding Topics.* September 16, 2022. https://explodingtopics.com/blog/smartphone-usage-stats.

James, Geoffrey. "45 Quotes From Mr. Rogers That We All Need Today." *Inc.* August 5, 2019. https://www.inc.com/geoffrey-james/45-quotes-from-mr-rogers-that-we-all-need-today.html.

Osman, Maddy. "Mind-blowing LinkedIn Statistics and Facts (2022)." *Kinsta.* October 21, 2022. https://kinsta.com/blog/linkedin-statistics/.

Chapter 6

Mackay, Harvey. "Mackay: When it comes to business, it is OK to have a little fun." *StarTribune.* May 24, 2021. https://www.startribune.com/when-it-comes-to-business-it-is-ok-to-have-a-little-fun/600060612/.

Chapter 7

Herrity, Jennifer. "How To Give an Elevator Pitch (With Examples)." Indeed.com. Last modified on August 26, 2022. https://www.indeed.com/career-advice/interviewing/how-to-give-an-elevator-pitch-examples.

"Two-Minute Commercial, aka "Elevator Speech."" University of North Texas Career Center Health Sciences. https://www.unthsc.edu/students/wp-content/uploads/sites/26/Interviewing_All.pdf.

Chapter 8

Centeno, Antonio. "How A Men's Dress Shirt Should Fit." *Business Insider.com* May 13, 2014. https://www.businessinsider.com/how-a-mens-dress-shirt-should-fit-2014-5.

Hajo, Adam and Adam D. Galinsky. (2012) "Enclothed cognition." *Journal of Experimental Social Psychology*, 48(4): 918-925. https://doi.org/10.1016/j.jesp.2012.02.008.

Louboutin, Christian. "Shoes transform your body language and attitude. They lift you physically and emotionally." Inspiring Quotes. https://www.inspiringquotes.us/author/1149-christian-louboutin.

Reiman, Tonya. *The Yes Factor.* 2010. New York, NY: Hudson Street Press.

Stillman, Jessica. "New Princeton Research: People Judge Your Competence Based on Your Clothes in Under 1 Second." *Inc. Magazine*, December 2019.

Trepanier, Dan. "How It Should Fit: The Jacket." *Blog: Articles of Style.* 2022.

Chapter 9

Golden, Shelley, Tieperman, Janice. "How to Look Good on Zoom." *wikiHow.com.* Last modified on September 1, 2022. https://www.wikihow.com/Look-Good-on-Zoom.

Chapter 10

Boskamp, Elsie. "21 Crucial Career Change Statistics [2022]: How Often Do People Change Jobs?" September 15, 2022. https://www.zippia.com/advice/career-change-statistics/.

ABOUT THE AUTHOR

Valerie Nifora's literary career had an inauspicious beginning. A daughter of Greek immigrant parents, Valerie's first language was not English. This hurdle hindered her in elementary school, but thanks to a teacher who insisted Valerie sit at the front of the room, she learned how to apply herself to her studies, eventually becoming an A student. That dedication to hard work carried her through high school and college and on to her career, and later on, a graduate degree.

For over twenty years, she has been a marketing communications leader for a Fortune 50. She has served as a ghostwriter for several executives and has executed award-winning campaigns using her special gift as a storyteller to inspire others. Her love of writing and creativity has earned her more than twenty awards throughout her career.

The awards are still coming her way through her published works. Valerie's book of romantic poetry, *I Asked the Wind*, was a Gold Award Winner from the Nonfiction Authors Association; Top 10 Finalist Global AEA Awards for Clean Romance, and Big NYC Book Awards

Distinguished Finalist, all in 2020. Her classic romance novel, *The Fairmounts*, was a #1 bestseller and #1 new release on Amazon in July and August of 2022. In October 2022, it won an Honorary Award by Academy Author Elite.

Valerie holds a B.A. in Communications from Emerson College and an M.B.A. from Fordham University. She is married and a mother of two amazing sons.

VALERIE WANTS TO CONNECT WITH YOU.

Valerie Nifora is an expert in all things personal branding.

Follow her on your favorite social media platforms and get inspired to be the best version of you!

ValerieNifora.com/PersonalBranding

HEATHER MONAHAN

Mastering
Your Beliefs, Actions,
and Knowledge
to Conquer Any
Adversity

OVERCOME
YOUR
VILLAINS

Overcome Your Villains will help you learn:

- Heather's 3-Step BAK process to evaluate your situation and identify a clear path forward.
- How to deal with (or overcome) a toxic environment, whether at work, at home, or in your own head.
- All the options to reach your full potential and how to start pursuing them.

For more information, visit HeatherMonahan.com

BLOCKCHAIN
VERIFIED IP™

Powered by Easy IP™

Made in the USA
Middletown, DE
11 July 2023